YOU HAD ONE JOB!

BEVERLY L. JENKINS

D0068176

Andrews McMeel
Publishing®

a division of Andrews McMeel Universal

YOU HAD ONE JOB!

INTRODUCTION

Chances are, you've made a mistake (or two!) at work before. It's OK; it happens. We're all human, after all. Yet sometimes those little mistakes come back to haunt you, especially now that everybody and their brother is armed with a cell phone camera and an Internet connection. This book is a celebration of all of those funny work-related blunders that you were hoping nobody would ever notice. Hung a street sign upside down? Somebody saw it. Forgot how to do basic addition? Saw it. Spelled something so terribly wrong that it hardly even looks like English anymore? Oh, they definitely saw that.

We're not judging; we're just laughing at how hard you failed at doing your job. OK, maybe we're judging you a little, but hey, you still got paid, right? Who's laughing now?

Credit: @tulky on Instagram

Breakfast at Fittany's.

Credit: Joshua Klee @joshedhs on Instagram

The bag may be screwed up, but you can bet that it's still filled with 75 percent air.

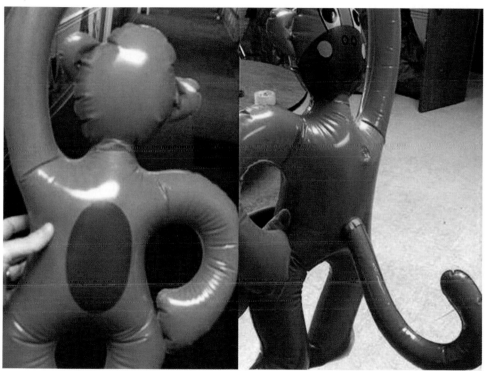

Credit: Thuisbezorgd on Imgur

Not a mistake. He's just happy to see us.

Credit: @cindyarco on Instagram

Two-hour wax? Who are you, Sasquatch?

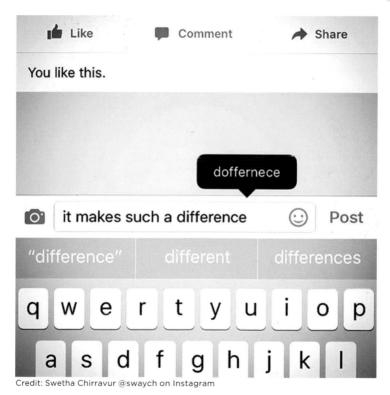

Credit: Swetha Chirravur @swaych on Instagram

Thanks, autocorrect. That's *really* helpful.

Credit: @talkmma on Instagram

Font choice is important. Just ask the residents of this street.

Credit: Hannah Bradshaw @hannahjams on Instagram

Sure it's ugly, but it works, so what's the problem?

Credit: AlderaanGaming on Imgur

I see you, orange Tic Tac.

Teenage Mutant Ninja Frozen? I'd watch that.

Credit: Ro Valencia @itshockeymom on Instagram

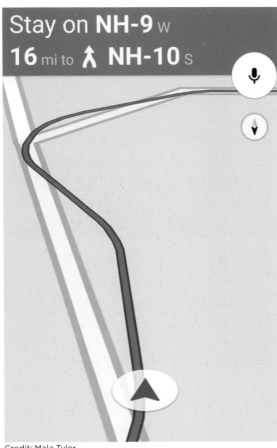

Go home, GPS. You're drunk.

Credit: Mala Tyler

Credit: Tim O'Neil @dankbluntage on Instagram

You know the drill: Say "in bed" after reading every fortune.

Credit: cindysrevenge on Imgur

That's helpful, thanks.

Credit: Joy Pobre @jchyld on Instagram

This is the sort of thing that gives people with OCD nightmares.

Credit: Sarah Jackson @sadahmae21 on Instagram

Obviously a typo. It should say "fat."

Credit: @fredbone62 on Instagram

I'm no doctor, but that can't be right.

Credit: John Dorr @dorrz_tat2z on Instagram

"Stencil? I don't need a stencil! I'm an artist."

Credit: @arch1tekt on Instagram

Look at the bright side: At least it's a "d" and not a "p."

Credit: @wickedsavvy on Instagram

All signs point to going back to bed.

Credit: Syed Othman Radhy AlSagoff @syedalsagoff92 on Instagram

My eye won't stop twitching when I look at this. That's normal, right?

Credit: Sunny Worthington @sunnyworthington

These are some odd cantaloupes, but so be it.

Credit: @therealphlegmeater on Instagram

Now that is classy. Is that a Van Gogh?

Credit: @j3ssi3d on Instagram

Was this written in that snake language from *Harry Potter*?

Credit: Kris Whalen @kriswithakbmx on Instagram

Sure, the city could fix this mistake . . . but where's the fun in that?

EXIT 119

No
Name
1/2 MILE

Naming things is hard. Just ask my son, Hey You.

Credit: Shawna Walsh @shawna_walsh on Twitter

When the real estate agent said the apartment had a balcony, she failed to mention one small detail.

Credit: @mohantyambarish_Twitter

Credit: Shaina Garcia @shai4699 on Instagram

Creamy, yes. Crunchy, not so much.

Lokay.

Credit: Kristin Mank @kmank95 on Imgur

Credit: Sandra Carrillo @fireflyqueen1 on Instagram

Something doesn't add up.

Credit: Sean Francis @thekat5150 on Instagram

It's not dumb if it works. Just kidding: This is still dumb.

Credit: Sighcopathic on Imgur

Donuts Dunkin' is the best!

Credit: David Elsenheimer @eheimer110389 on Instagram

On second thought, I think I'll just take the bus.

Credit: Ryan Price @fourthrook on Instagram

Safety first: Always look through the peephole before answering your door.

Credit: Valerie Caruso

Where is this Mex Canada you speak of? Can you point it out on a map?

Credit: @gnegis on Instagram

And Happy Airthday to you, as well.

Credit: @ramone_mayo on Instagram

Proofreaders? Who needs 'em?

Credit: @hollyjanetowers on Instagram

Fashion is confusing.

Credit: @joshuamichaeltx on Instagram

You can't get from point A to point B without point C.

Credit: @nhemann on Instagram

Shart removal is serious business.

Credit: Chris Sutherland @chrissuds

How many leather products must they sell to afford a new sign?

Credit: FuManLu on Imgur

Well you know, it's impossible to build things around trees. They're always moving around so much!

Credit: Dan Jenkins

Raw on the inside, burned on the outside—
just like Mom used to make!

Credit: Paul Mitchell @pauldarcymitchell on Instagram

Is it supposed to burn like this?

Credit: MagnusMan on Imgur

Yet another unrealistic body standard that we can never live up to, right, ladies?

Credit: @simondell on Instagram

Small car? Uh, yeah.

Credit: Brit Morris @brattneymorris on Instagram

Be right back; I have a job application to drop off.

Credit: Angela Osborn @mrsangosborn on Instagram

Measure twice, cut once? Who's got time for that?

Credit: Phil Simmons @ed1951 on Instagram

Who wants a nice slice of my dump cake?
Anyone? Anyone?

Credit: Felix Reyes @farsys on Instagram

Yeah, happy bertday! (Just be glad it's not a dump cake.)

Credit: @radiotoast on Instagram

When I think of lipstick, my mind immediately jumps to fine cheese.

Credit: @taltybit on Instagram

These aren't the warts you're looking for. Also, why are you looking for warts? That's gross.

Credit: Ty Wynn @bustersocks on Instagram

Close enough.

"We are better at installing car parts than signs, we swear."

Credit: Drake Wilson @sauron14

You shall not pass.

Credit: Arie Tri Sandy @tigasandy on Instagram

Credit: Chaunte Flores @itsmechaunte

These bears are still in the embryo phase.

It's a good thing they put the exhaust hood over the sink. That water can get really hot!

Credit: cliffy23 on Imgur

Credit: @OMGitsADDYB on Twitter

"Gloden Bronge" is totally your color.

Credit: @tycer_tank on Instagram

I always thought making someone's sh*t list was a *bad* thing.

Let's just hope this isn't a fire exit.

Credit: Gil D. Faingezicht @gfaingezicht on Instagram

This tricky label allows you to read it while drinking. It's just clever marketing, that's all.

Credit: Tara McKinney-@taramckinney70

They call this the "I got dressed in the car on the way here" look.

Credit: Jenny Shiel Sanchez Bongolan @jennybieable

Credit: theguvnorj on Instagram

I would, but I don't even know what "claer" means.

Credit: @frenchie758 on Instagram

Suddenly there's a line stretching all the way around the block.

Credit: @jadedgirl369 on Instagram

This is a commitment to laziness that you just don't see every day. Bravo.

Credit: mijosm on Imgur

Thanks, but I prefer my coffee not freshly, if that's okay.

Credit: @jazzpatron on Instagram

"Hello, Quality Control? We have a problem."

Credit: @josabella14 on Instagram

And that's when we knew the road crews were trying to kill us.

Credit: Kevin Dudginski @bigkevind on Instagram

Little Jane didn't pay attention during her basic grammar lessons. Don't be like Jane.

Credit: jewlynn on Imgur

Knock knock. Who's there?
Fired. Fired who?
You are. You're fired. Now get out.

Credit: Sue Fairchild @suefair48 on Instagram

This watermelon would be great if it weren't for all the splinters.

Credit: @T_Qif on Twitter

Don't stare at his nose. Just . . . don't.

Credit: @ja_nellie_bean on Instagram

That's not road work; it's modern art.

Credit: Andy Moody @andyjmoody on Instagram

I dare you to bounce it off the backboard.

Credit: @sea_again_rkpt on Instagram

I hope your day brings some unexpected spice.
If you're into that sort of thing.

Credit: Zachary Carter @zagir44 on Instagram

But what if I don't have any thinks to give?

Credit: Emil Hoff on Imgur

You can't expect city workers to know how to spell their city's name. That's crazy talk.

Credit: @t_whittington on Instagram

"But it was on sale!"
—Some husband, somewhere.

Credit: Lion James @lion6015 on Instagram

Tear here, tear there. Tear anywhere, really, just give me my darn ketchup.

Credit: Rebekah @farmwife23

Stay in csohol, kids. No, really.

Credit: @will_peeters on Instagram

For the ramp user who craves adventure,
not to mention a challenge.

Credit: @smurfette__89 on Instagram

No thanks, I'll pass. I like to maintain a low printer ink diet.

Credit: @pup_nyx on Instagram

He didn't attend four years of medical school to be called MISTER Seuss.

Credit: Steven Shogan @stevenshogan on Instagram

Here we have a permanent reminder of the day Bill got chased by bees while painting the street lines.

Credit: Yoni Limor @yonimation on Instagram

Which way to the restoom?

Credit: Jen Ashley @LionDuckling on Twitter

Really, here? Well, okay. [unzips pants]

Credit: Per Silvergren

Sanil the snail wants to help kids to reed gud.

Credit: Sundi @jahzara on Instagram

Certainly looks official. Better do what the misspelled spray-painted sign says.

Credit: Tailor Pribis @littlemisstai66 on Instagram

Oh, you didn't want privacy in the *restroom*, did you? Privacy shmivacy!

RASPBERRY

BANANA

Credit: @thugmestic on Instagram

It's time to give this store clerk a raise.

Credit: @LMFrederick on Instagram

Oh yeah, you're a genius all right. Move over, Stephen Hawking.

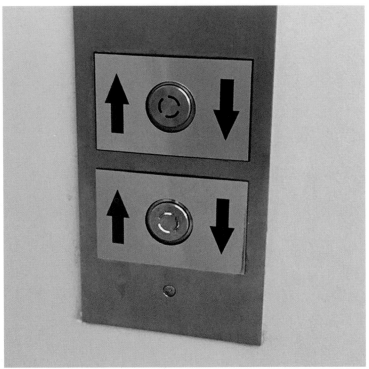

Credit: Christina Austin @missfit_chriss33 on Instagram

I give up. I'll just stay here.

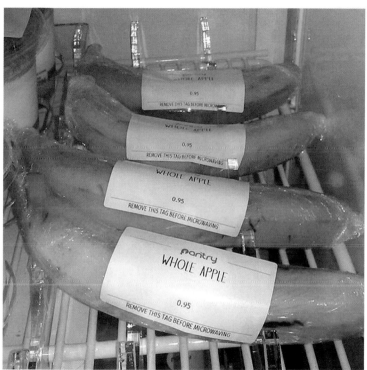

Credit: @vejarjonny on Instagram

There are so many things wrong here.

reg.   sale
$40.00   **$16.00**
$44.00   **$17.60**
$48.00   **$19.20**
$50.00   **$20.00**

50% off
Canyon River Blues
fleece tops

Credit: Rebecca Heinrich @rheinrich02 on Instagram

Math is hard.

Credit: Martin Casey @martbar6 on Instagram

"Come on up" or "Please leve alone?"
WHICH IS IT?

"Um . . . I meant to do that?"

Credit: Miriam Buehrer on Imgur

Credit: Reanell Selina @totaldivarea

"Martha! This milk has spoiled!"

Credit: Ryan Sanborn @ryanpippinsanborn on Instagram

Must be for *Star Wars X: Attack of the Hufflepuffs.*

Credit: @maxinads on Instagram

This sign manages to be both oddly specific and completely useless. Kudos.

Going down . . . er, sideways?

Credit: Sandy Simpson @punkyjanejewelry on Instagram

This sign is obviously incorrect. It should say, "Buy more, save LESS."

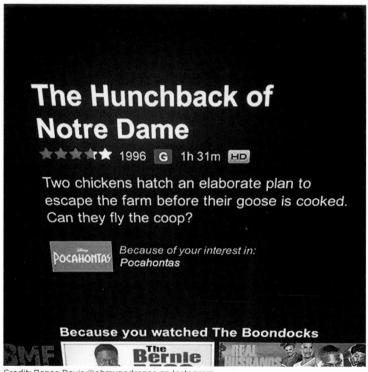

The Hunchback of Notre Dame

★★★★★ 1996 G 1h 31m HD

Two chickens hatch an elaborate *plan to* escape the farm before their goose is *cooked.* Can they fly the coop?

POCAHONTAS *Because of your interest in:*
Pocahontas

Because you watched The Boondocks

Credit: Renee Davis @ohmygodrenee on Instagram

"Netflix and Chill" night just got weird.

Credit: Becca Alley @iamtheknight234 on Instagram

No wonder they're closing.

Credit: @ednheaven on Instagram

A for effort. F for execution.

These sprinkles are made of LIES.

Credit: Megan Bliss

Credit: @jennfreaxx on Instagram

Little-known fact: Under that Jedi robe Yoda was RIPPED.

Credit: Leah Dorion @leahj1978 on Instagram

Which way to Warman? If only there was some kind of sign. . . .

Credit: Andy Parrish @andy351_1999 on Instagram

The counter gets nice and dry. Your hands, not so much.

Credit: @zahinemtiyaz on Instagram

"I do what I want."

Credit: Rick Loy @lionoloy on Instagram

You can always count on the NFL for a high-quality wascloth.

Credit: @tohtua on Instagram

Somebody really stinks at jigsaw puzzles.

Credit: @djargent2003 on Twitter

Whoever designed this bathroom clearly knows how much men like to get chummy while taking a whiz.

Credit: @wonderland_dreaming97 on Instagram

A nice refreshing bottle of BBQ sauce always hits the spot while exercising.

Credit: @x_coley_x on Instagram

No, sir, it does not. Absolutely not. Don't even ask it to, because the answer is no.

Credit: @ninja_warrior_princess on Instagram

I never thought I'd have an existentialist dilemma in a parking garage, yet here we are.

Credit: Richard Diaz @ric_0_5uave on Instagram

It's like they're trying to communicate with us, but I'm just not getting it.

Credit: raywoloszyn on Instagram and @Barbaro1420 on Twitter

There is such a thing as being too literal.

Credit: @sherrilmetal on Instagram

That's not retro; it's just backwards.

Credit: Matt Walpole @mattwalpole on Twitter

Last I checked, exposing yourself on a street corner was frowned upon.

Credit: Jim Jenkins

Just think: These are the guys you call when something's broken.

Credit: Joan Falconer

What gave me away?
Was it the horns?

Credit: Danielle Adams @makenasmommi on Instagram

You didn't really want beets anyway.

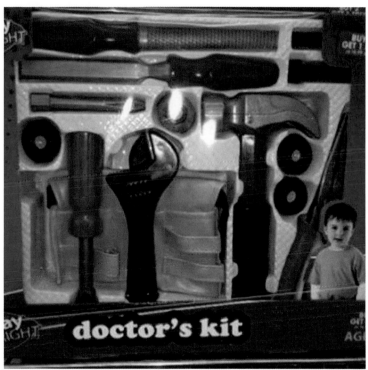

Credit: cindysrevenge on Imgur

Dr. Sawbones will see you now.

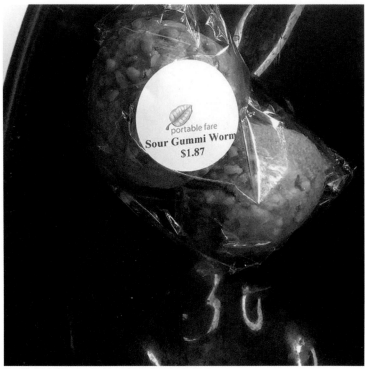

Credit: Cody Snyder @obiwankenodi on Instagram

I don't recall gummi worms being this doughy, but whatever you say.

Credit: Sammy B @s_a_m_o_s_a

These store clerks knew *exactly* what they were doing.

I'd make a joke, but it would be corny.

Credit: @moluxnova on Instagram

Credit: Dew M. Chaiyanara @dewmewmew on Instagram

Arguing is the BEST part of teatime.

WHERE SHOPPING IS A PLEASURE

1 99 LB

NAME

Credit: u-hateburn on Imgur

Do you ever feel like you're forgetting to do something?

Credit: John Reis @johncutsvideo on Instagram

This packaging is highly illogical.

Up to 55% Off Grass-Fed Steak Sampler

~~$277.79~~
$129

Credit: April McNamara @aprilmariemc on Instagram

Nothing like a nice juicy steak. (No really, this is NOTHING like a nice juicy steak.)

Credit: Sergio Mercado @liverpoolreject91 on Instagram

This sign just screams: "Put your life in our hands! We're worthy of your trust!"

Credit: Kate Broadhurst @shenamedmemaeve on Instagram

Blatant false advertising.

Credit: Marcus Sullivan @newviewdesigns on Instagram

"Open all the time, except when we're closed."

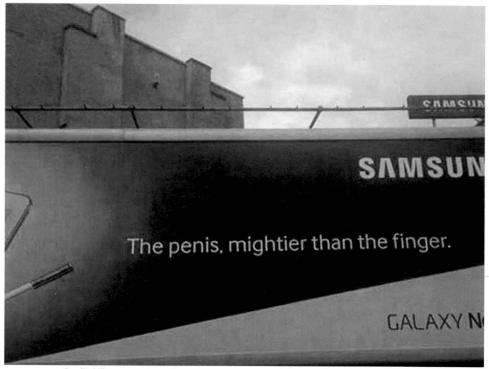

Credit: killnaytor on Imgur

Depends on whom you ask.

When putting sliced bread in a bag is too challenging for you, it might be time to find a new line of work.

Credit: wastedalldaythinkingofnothing on Imgur

Credit: Luis-Lugardo @no_crossfire

Clearance for what? An upside-down, low-flying airplane?

Credit: @dadutchess22 on Instagram

Ribbit.

Credit: @vivaladanniella on Instagram

Oh, we're sorry, too. We're all sorry.

Credit: Adam Wilson @willies_place on Instagram

Let me just swing by the ATM.

YOU HAD ONE JOB!

Andrews McMeel Publishing

a division of Andrews McMeel Universal

1130 Walnut Street, Kansas City, Missouri 64106

www.andrewsmcmeel.com

16 17 18 19 20 SDB 10 9 8 7 6 5 4 3 2 1

ISBN: 978-1-4494-7969-5

Library of Congress Control Number: 2016931071

EDITOR: Megan Sinclair
DESIGNER: Diane Marsh
ART DIRECTOR: Diane Marsh
COPY CHIEF: Maureen Sullivan
PRODUCTION MANAGER: Carol Coe
DEMAND PLANNER: Sue Eikos

ATTENTION: SCHOOLS AND BUSINESSES
Andrews McMeel books are available at quantity discounts
with bulk purchase for educational, business, or sales
promotional use. For information, please e-mail the Andrews
McMeel Publishing Special Sales Department:
specialsales@amuniversal.com.